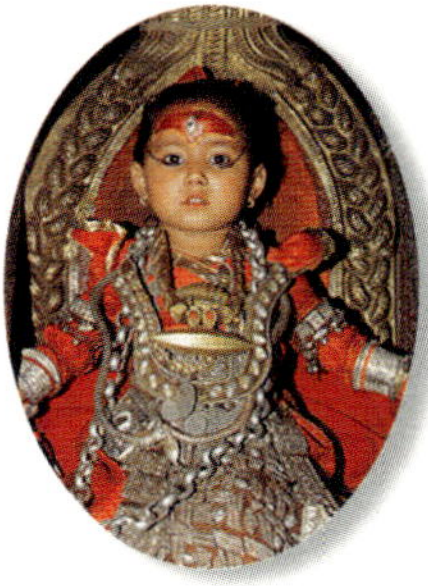

KUMARI

the virgin goddess

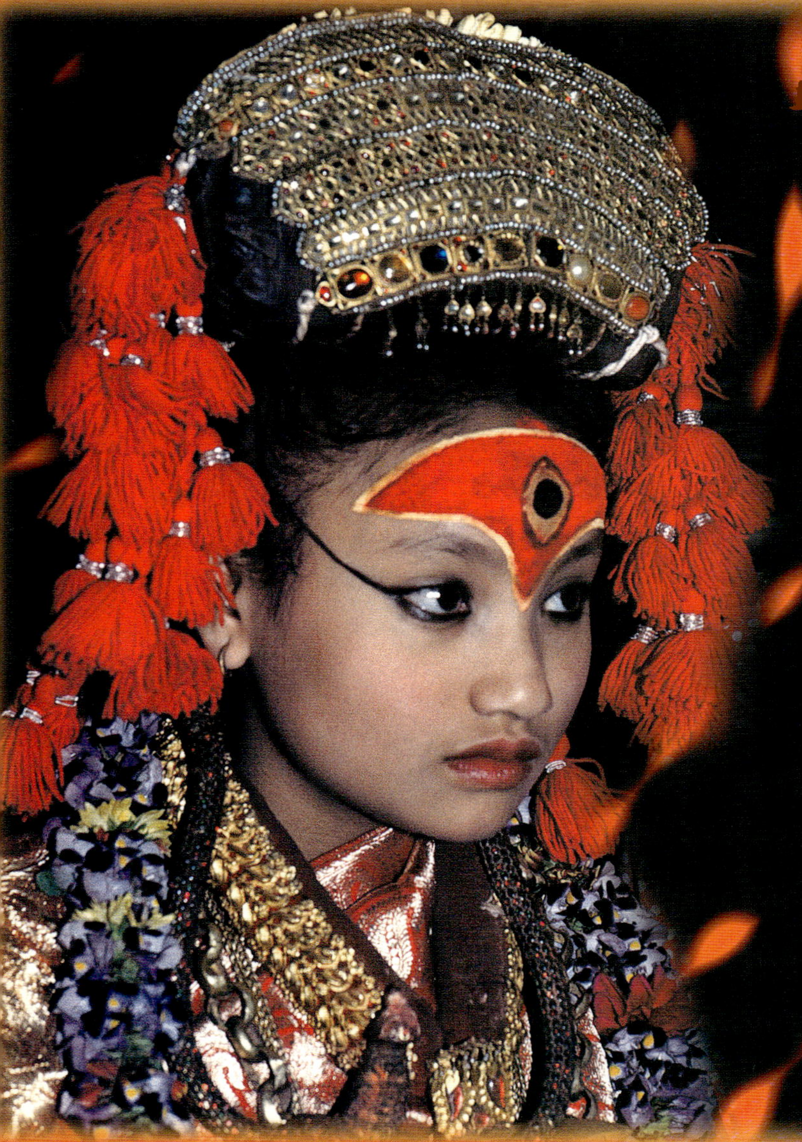

KUMARI

the virgin goddess

Text:
Carroll Dunham
Daniel B. Haber

Photographs:
Thomas L. Kelly

Lustre Press
Roli Books

A doll-like face with ruby lips and elongated painted eyes, with a third eye painted on her red forehead, appears from behind a carved wooden window. 'Is that her? That little girl?' A woman with a strong New York accent questions incredulously in the courtyard below.

Resembling a figure from a Mughal miniature painting, the little girl, not more than five years old, dressed in regal red, peering through eyes blackened with kohl, solemnly gazes down from her window at the gaping crowd without uttering a word.

'Ladies and gentlemen,' a priest announces, 'she is Kumari, the Living Goddess. Please applaud.' The pious Nepalese clap along with the gawking, camera-toting tourists who throng the Kumari's palace in the heart of Kathmandu's historic Durbar Square, near the old Royal Palace.

Within a few moments, however, the little 'goddess' withdraws. One European lady, visibly moved, comments, 'She had an expressionless look on her face. As she looked out at the people, her eyes met mine for about two seconds, and my heart stood still. After all, I had just looked into the eyes of a living goddess. I feel that I have been deeply blessed!'

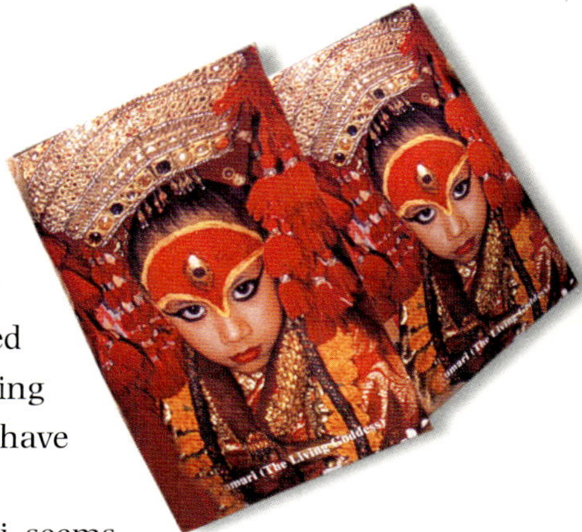

A young girl hides behind the Kumari's mask.

The Royal Kumari seems to lead a fairytale existence. However, shrouded with the secrecy associated with tantric rituals, and taught from an early age that a goddess is to utter as few words as possible, the inner feelings of a Kumari remain as mysterious and inaccessible as a deity made of stone.

Moreover not just any Nepalese girl can become a Kumari. The present Kumari was chosen in 2001 at the tender age of four. 'She was screened by the royal astrologer, many priests, and the King's religious advisor,' her father boasts. She was also inspected by female attendants for the necessary thirty-two perfections of a goddess. These include clear skin with small pores, even teeth, black hair and eyes, soft hands, a moist tongue, and no offensive body odours. She must have 'thighs like a deer, a chest like a lion, neck like a conch shell, eyelashes like a cow, and a body like a banyan tree.' Most importantly, she must show no signs of ever having shed menstrual blood, for that would signify the end of her reign as a living goddess.

The Kumaris are enthroned with great fanfare. They traditionally belong to the Newar Buddhist community, and the residents of the Kathmandu Valley have worshipped them for nearly 700 years as the living incarnations of the Hindu goddess Taleju Bhawani, the mythological protectress of the king and the people of the Himalayan kingdom.

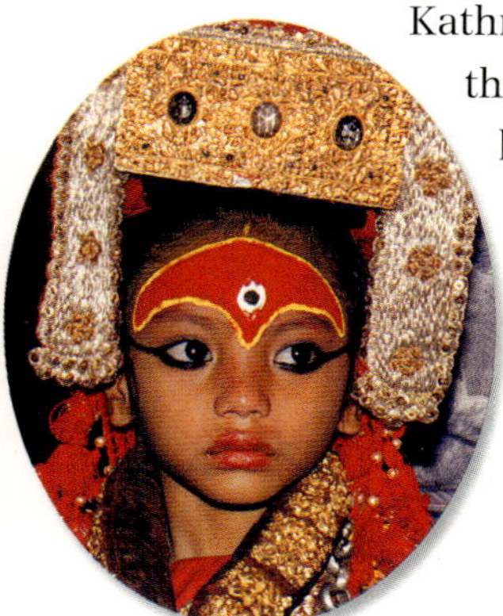

The third eye is painted on the forehead.

According to legend, the ravishing goddess and the king of the Malla dynasty were so intimate that the goddess would appear to him in human form, advising him on matters of state. They even played dice together in secret chambers of the adjacent Royal Palace. One day, however, overcome by lust during a game of dice, the king made an improper advance and the goddess vanished into thin air, saying she would never return. The king pleaded with her in vain. One day she appeared to him in a dream and told him to select a virgin girl whose body she could inhabit, and construct a separate Kumari Ghar in which she could reside. The present Kumari Ghar or Kumari Bahal was constructed in A.D. 1757 by Jaya Prakash Malla. Another version of the story is that the king had raped and murdered a pre-pubescent girl, and to atone for his sins, he began the practice of installing a young virgin as a living goddess and worshipping her.

When the Kumari attains puberty, the search for a new living goddess begins. Five priests conduct the search for a likely candidate from amongst the gold and silversmith families of the Buddhist Sakya clan, into which the Buddha was born as Prince Siddhartha 2,500 years ago.

The short-listed candidates then have to spend a night in a murky chamber piled with severed buffalo heads, still bloody from the sacrifices of Dasain when hundred and eight beasts are ritually decapitated. The girl who endures this ghastly trial with equanimity is considered the suitable embodiment of the goddess. Installed through an occult ritual in the Taleju temple, the spirit of the goddess gradually possesses her young body to become the Living Goddess or *Deomaiju* in Newari.

Some consider the Kumari to be the incarnation of the virgin goddess Kanya Kumari, one of the names given to Parvati, the consort of Lord Shiva, who in his form of Pashupatinath, is the presiding deity of the Hindu kingdom. The current Kumari is called the Royal Kumari, to distinguish her from past Kumaris and others who are worshipped in different parts of the Kathmandu valley. Once astrologers are satisfied that the Kumari's horoscope is in harmony with that of the king's, she is settled into the Kumari Bahal.

The Kumari lives alone in the ornate, recently restored 18th-century, doll-house palace. Her daily schedule varies little. Attendants set her hair in a ritual bun; her eyes are rimmed with black soot from a sacred butter lamp extending like a Zen painter's stroke to her temples, while her forehead is distinctively painted with a vermilion, red, black and golden all-seeing 'fire-eye'. Each day she sits on her throne for two or three hours, during which a priest from the nearby Taleju temple performs a purification rite, using objects said to cleanse each sensory organ: flour for the ears, rice for the mouth, incense for the nose, a lamp for the eyes and red powder for touch.

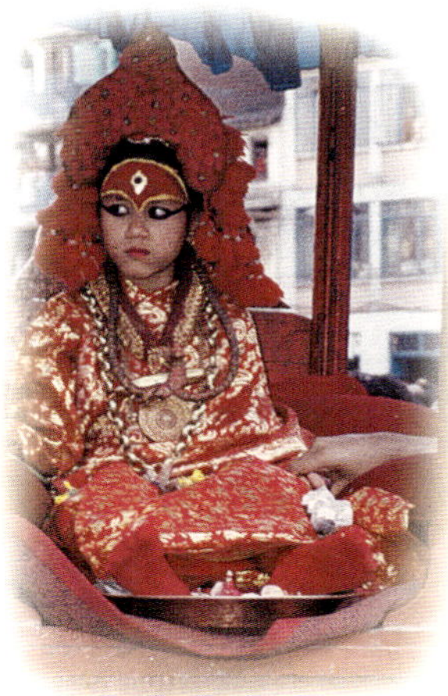

A Kumari from Kathmandu

The Kumari receives up to a dozen devotees every day. Her attendant adds, 'Some come with medical problems, especially illnesses related to bleeding. Many government officials visit, hoping her blessings will ensure a promotion.' The little goddess must remain solemn and silent, sitting cross-legged on her gilt-canopied lion throne, while worshippers shuffle through her private chamber, touching the floor with their heads, and laying down offerings of rupees, fruits or flowers. To them every micro-movement she makes is deemed a sign from Goddess Taleju. If she receives a petition in unmoved silence, it signals fulfillment; should she laugh, cry or rub her eyes, the supplicant could fall ill or even die.

Now in her early twenties, Anita Shakya was the Royal

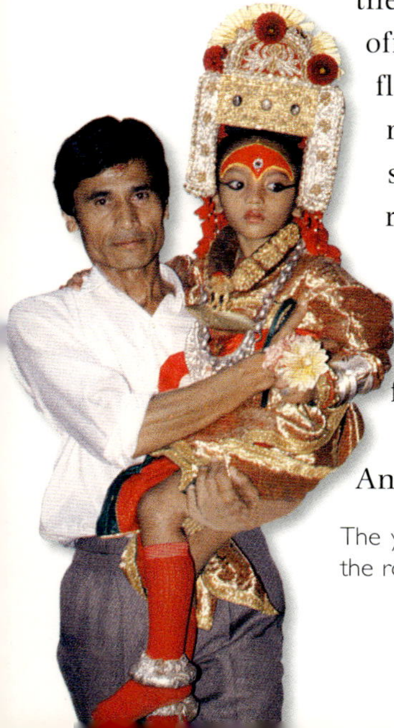

The young virgin goddess is being carried to the royal Kumari Ghar in Kathmandu.

Kumari a decade ago. Shy and reserved, as most ex-Kumaris are, she relates a sad story. 'I was a little girl. Once an old, sick man came to me to be blessed. He was coughing and a droplet of spittle landed on one of my toes. My attendants gasped in horror. The old man died the next day. I felt very sad, as I believed I was responsible for his death.'

For all the aura of mystique that surrounds her, the Kumari's only companions are an elderly hereditary chaperone, nannies and their children, a Hindu Brahmin *pujari* and a dozen Buddhist priests. Previous Kumaris remained illiterate but the present incumbent has been enrolled in Kathmandu's Raktakali School and receives private lessons at home. The government has increased her monthly allowance to Rs. 6,000, and the Royal Palace pays Rs. 3,000 for private lessons. Like other Nepalese children her age, she plays carom and video games with the caretakers' children, but only within her silk-draped chambers as she is forbidden to go out into the sunlight.

She survives on a strict diet and wakes up early every morning to spend hours at her devotions. Her original name and identity are buried; the priest tells her she is beyond joy and sorrow, as she is now a deity in human form. She is told that if she weeps or laughs, the deity will leave her.

'When I was Kumari I would look out of the window at all the children playing. I wanted to play too,' laments Dil Kumari, a grey-haired woman whose tenure as a living goddess ended over forty years ago. 'I wanted to be like a butterfly and fly down to join the playing children. I used to play stones and jacks all by myself.'

Nani Maya, another former Kumari, on the other hand, happily recalls: 'I have such fond memories of my time as a Kumari,' she says. 'I loved the caretakers at the Kumari Ghar more than my own family. I still go and visit the present Kumari and her attendants almost every week.'

After the summer monsoons, Kathmandu celebrates the end of the four-month rainy season with Indrajatra, a joyous festival honouring Lord Indra, the demigod of the rains, who is propitiated for good harvests. After all, Nepal is essentially an agrarian society dependant on a good rice crop. Arguably the most spectacular of the Valley festivals, Indrajatra is celebrated by the raising of a fifty-foot ceremonial phallic pole, accompanied by torch-lit processions and jubilant dancing in the streets. The week-long celebrations centre around Hanuman Dhoka or the Gate of Hanuman at the old Royal Palace in Durbar Square. On the third day, the Kumari is ceremoniously carried to her special chariot for a parade—her divine feet may not touch the ground—and she is worshipped by the king.

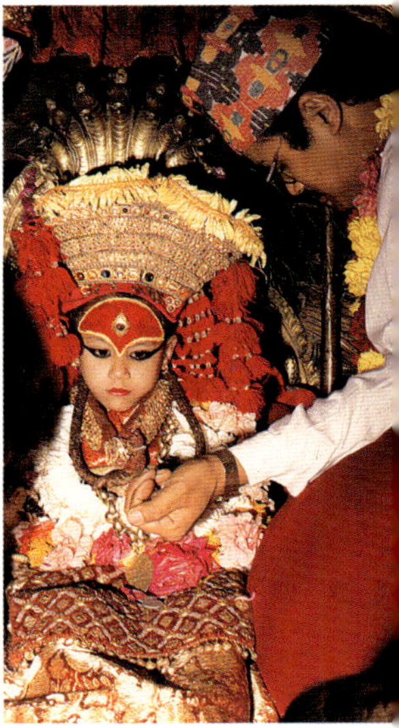

Nepalese kings have been worshipping Kumaris since the seventeenth century.

A glittering moment, this is the highlight of each year. But fairytales must end, and little girls, even goddesses, grow up. One cannot stay a Kumari forever. With the first shedding of blood, the deity Taleju is said to leave the child's body, returning her once more to the mundane world. Worshipped one last time in the company of the new Kumari, she is stripped of all her ornaments and taken back by twenty guardians and priests to her family home that she barely knows.

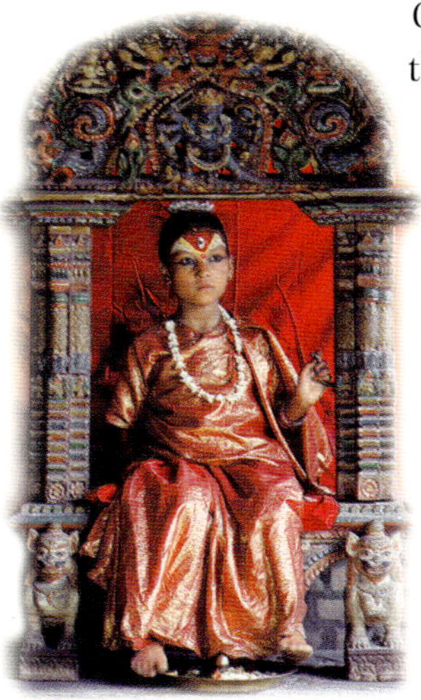

Once worshipped as divine, the young girl suddenly has to adapt to being treated as a ritually impure menstruating girl. After four days in isolation in a dark room with no sunlight, female attendants of the Taleju temple undo the little girl's ceremonial hair bun and remove her last token

The royal Kumari on her throne

bangle, signifying her re-entry into life as a mortal with feet of clay.

Several ex-Kumaris have had a hard time adjusting to normal life. Weaned on pomp and leisure, they are expected to cook, clean and do other menial chores. A former Kumari, Dil Kumari, recalls the hardship of returning home and having to quickly adjust to an arranged marriage and the burdens of being a housewife. 'Married life was difficult after being treated like a deity. As a daughter-in-law I had to obey my in-laws; as a wife, I had to obey my husband. I was accustomed to people worshipping me and bringing me gifts.'

Another problem in the old days was that few Nepalese men wanted to marry a dethroned goddess. According to old wives' tales, serpents were said to issue forth from their vaginas, devouring weak husbands. Out of nine recent ex-Kumaris, seven married, and their husbands subsequently died within the first year of marriage.

But times are changing, somewhat for the

better. Not all Kumaris are destined to lives marked by trauma. Former Royal Kumari Nani Maya, a generation later, is now a well-adjusted, happily married middle-aged housewife and mother of two who runs her own pharmacy. She says, 'I feel blessed to have been a Kumari. It was a real privilege. But my husband feels otherwise. When the priests asked us to offer our daughter, he refused. He would rather see our daughter receive a good education.'

'We need Kumaris; no goddess is more important to this valley,' insists Siddhi Laxmi, the septuagenarian mother of Patan's Dharma Kumari, the oldest and longest-serving Kumari in the Kathmandu Valley, enthroned in 1953. According to Juju Bhai Sakya, a leading proponent of the system, the tradition will continue as long as families of the Sakya clan continue to send their young daughters to become Kumaris.

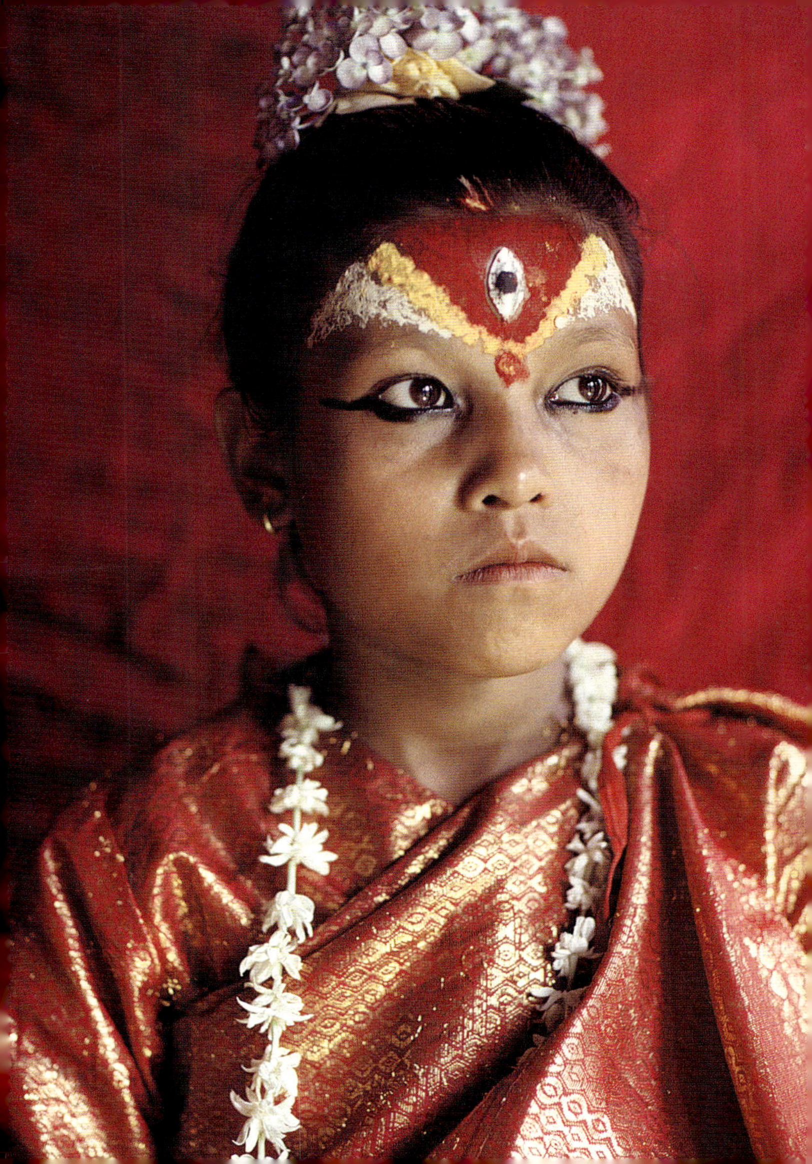

■ *Not just any girl can become a Kumari. She is required, first of all, to be a virgin and is then inspected for the '32 perfections' of a goddess: from a clear complexion to a moist tongue.*

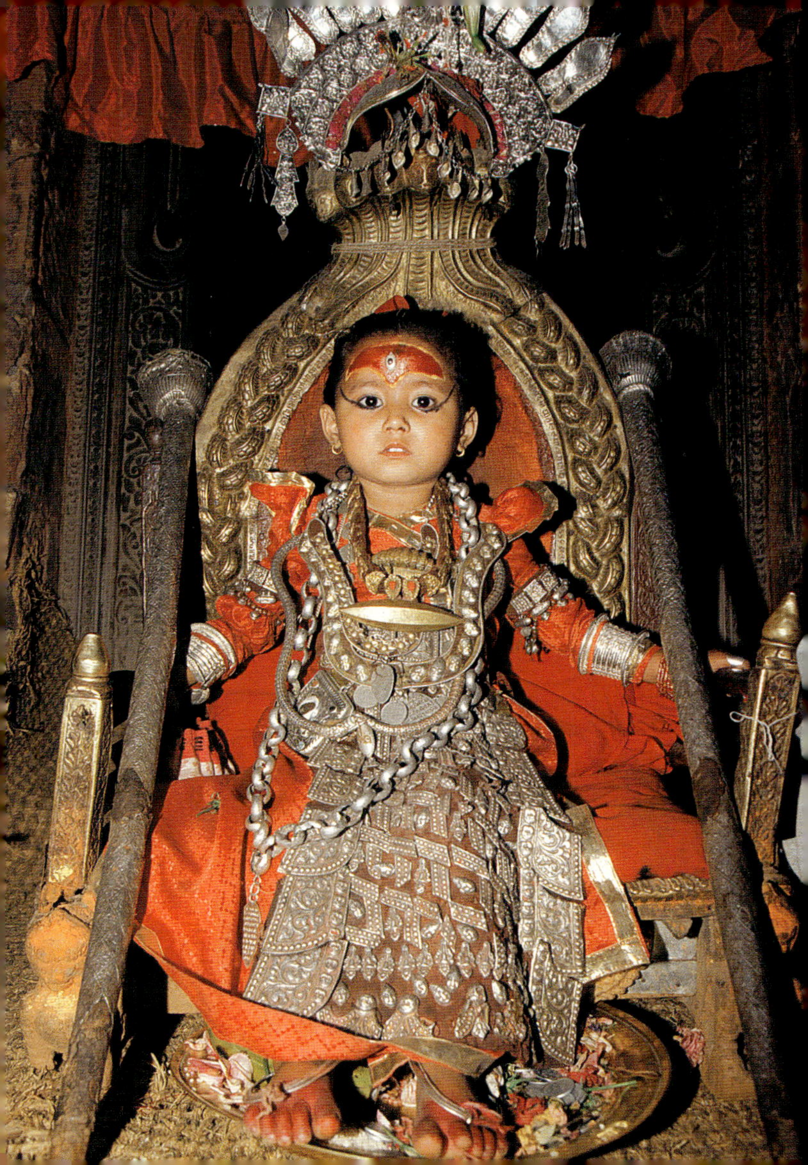

■ *The Kumari sits on her throne for at least two to three hours daily. She is heavily dolled up: her eyes rimmed with kohl, a 'fire-eye' painted on her forehead, with a regal red dress hiding her young body.*

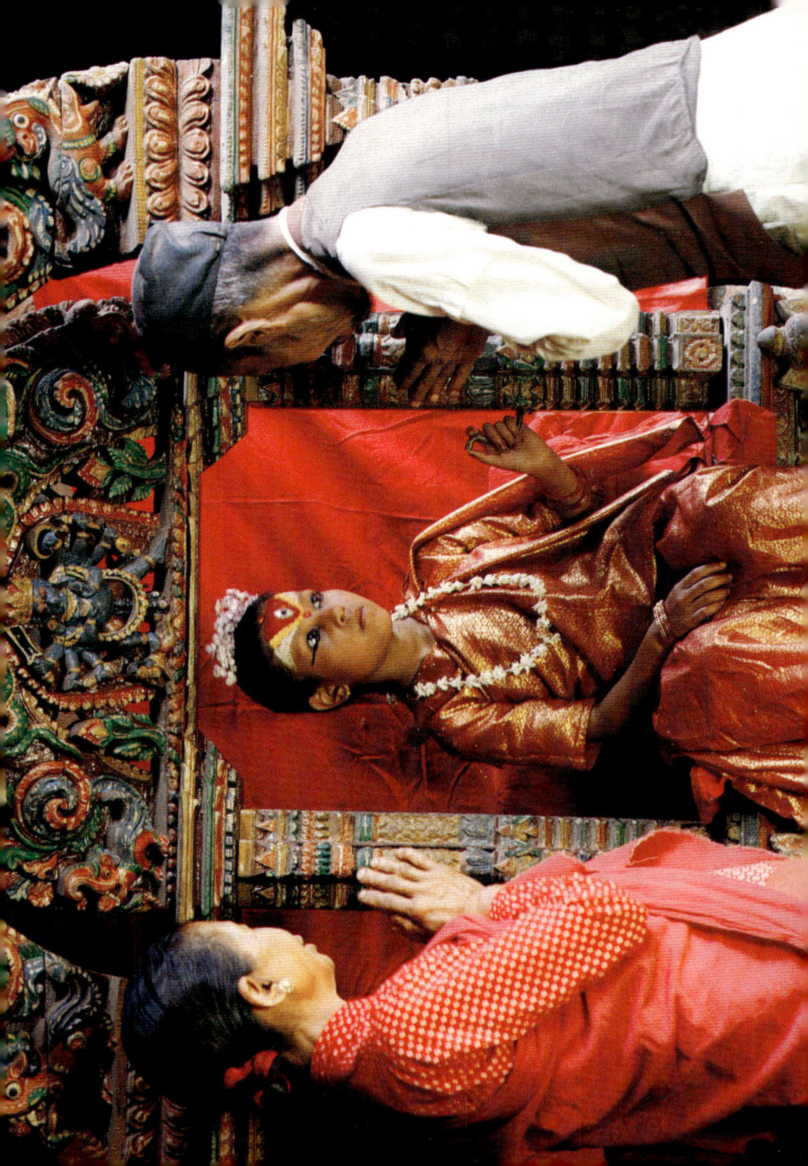

■ *While granting audience, the Kumari sits completely still. Any movement she makes is immediately interpreted as a sign from Goddess Taleju herself.*

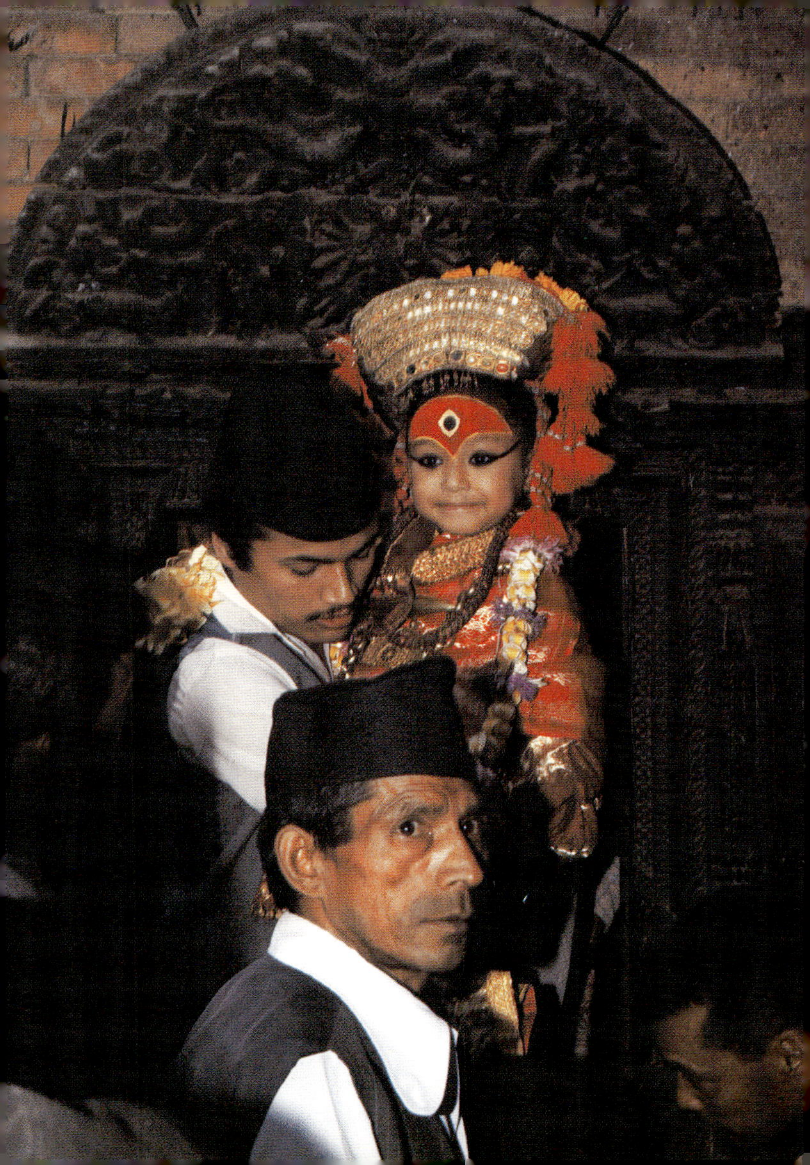

■ *Though Goddess Taleju is a Hindu deity, the royal Kumari is always chosen from the Newar Buddhist Sakya caste of goldsmiths and silversmiths.*

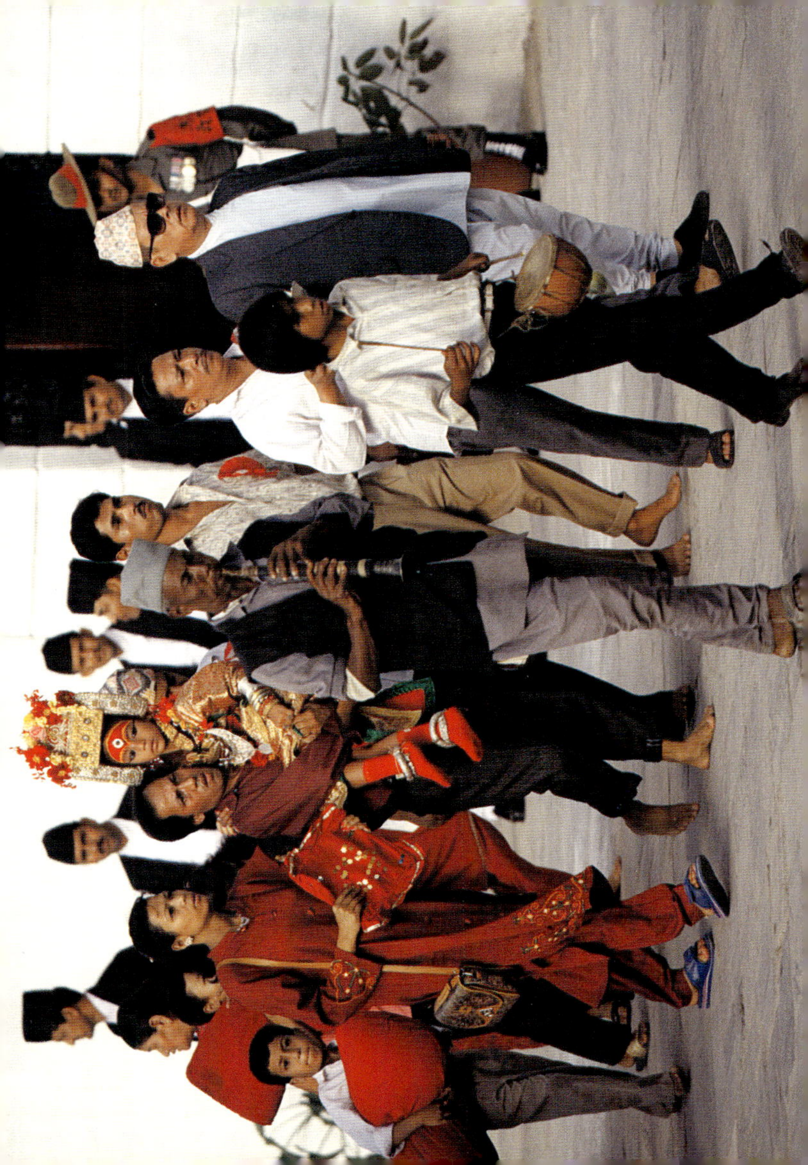

■ *The royal Kumari being taken in a procession to the restored eighteenth-century Kumari Ghar in Kathmandu.*

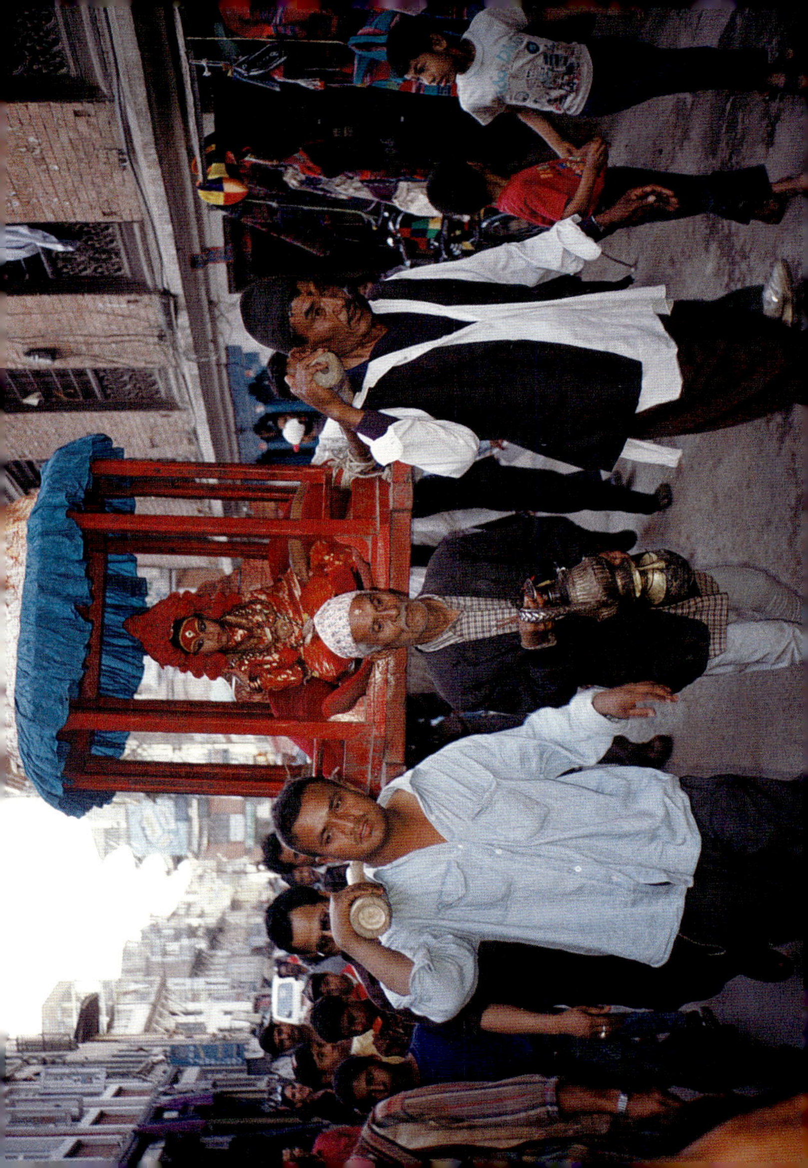

■ *The Kumari is being carried on a hand-held carriage by her numerous devotees. Her status in Nepal as a living goddess remains assured.*

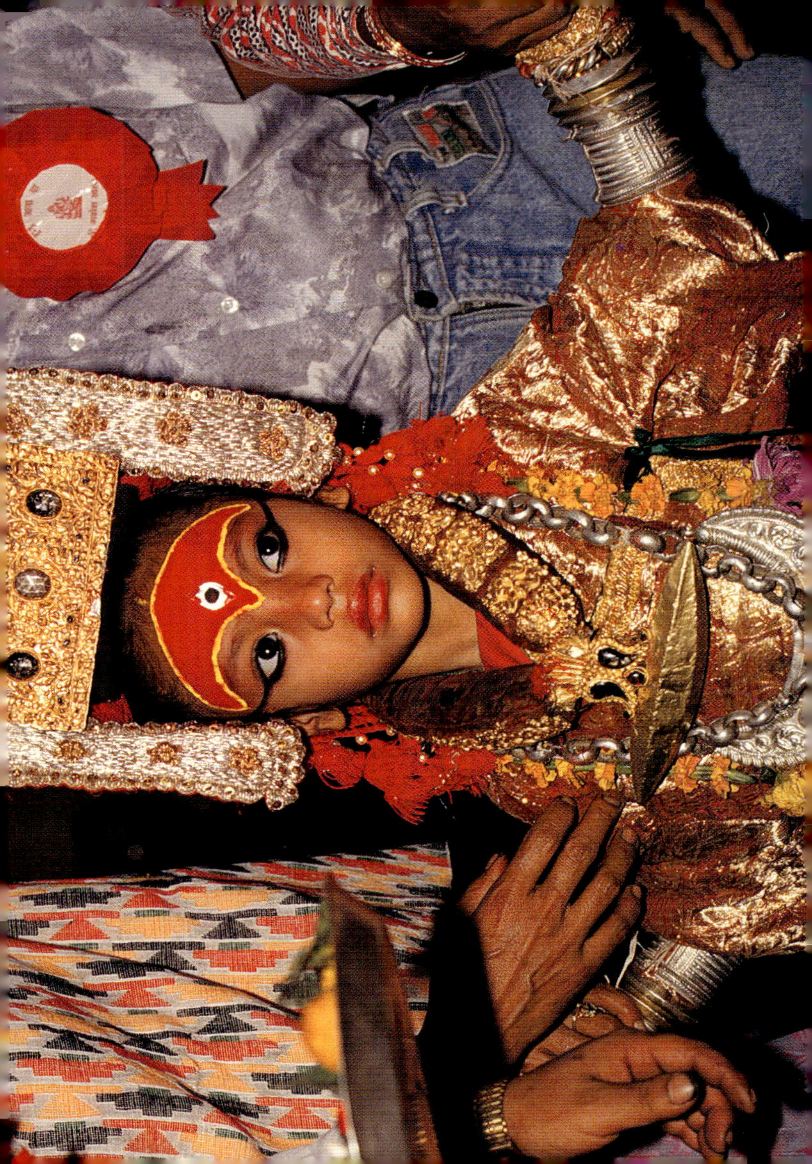

■ *A thick aura of mystique surrounds the Kumari. But hers is a lonely existence, denied the rights of childhood and the joys of playfulness.*

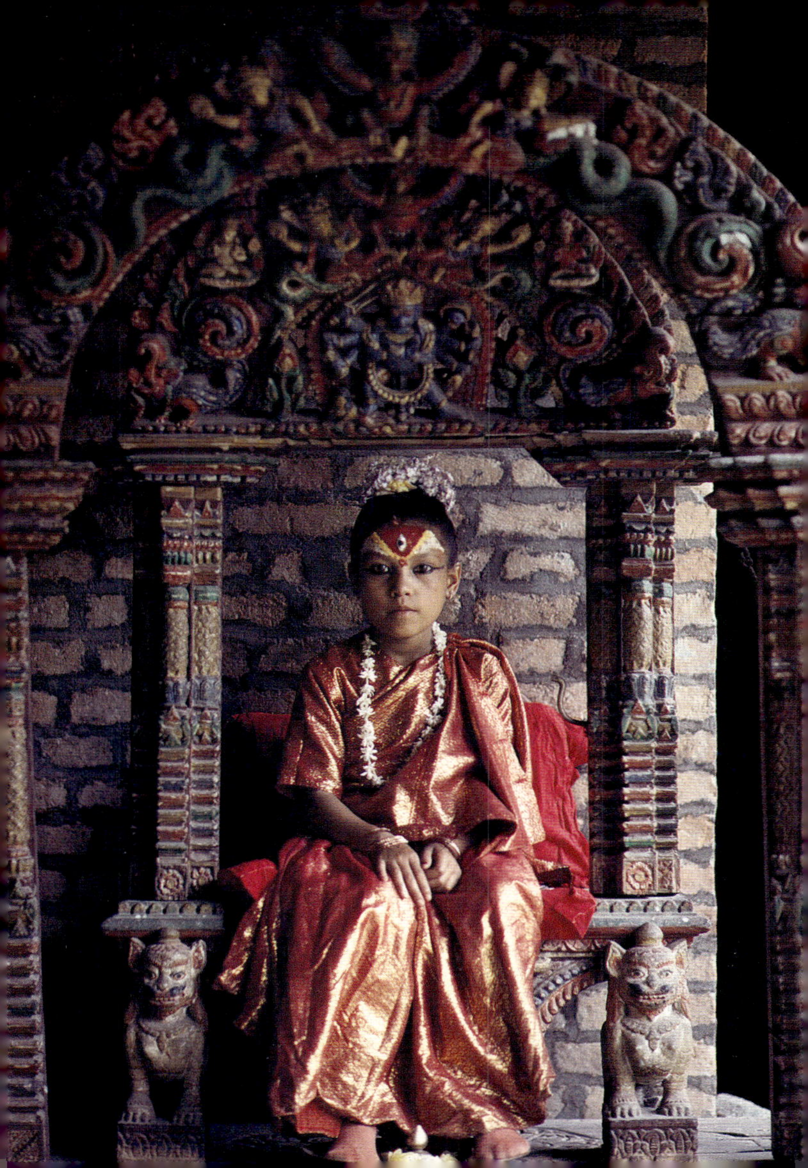

■ *Kumaris, the living virgin goddesses, come from three of the most important townships of Kathmandu valley in Nepal – Patan, Kathmandu and Bhaktapur.*

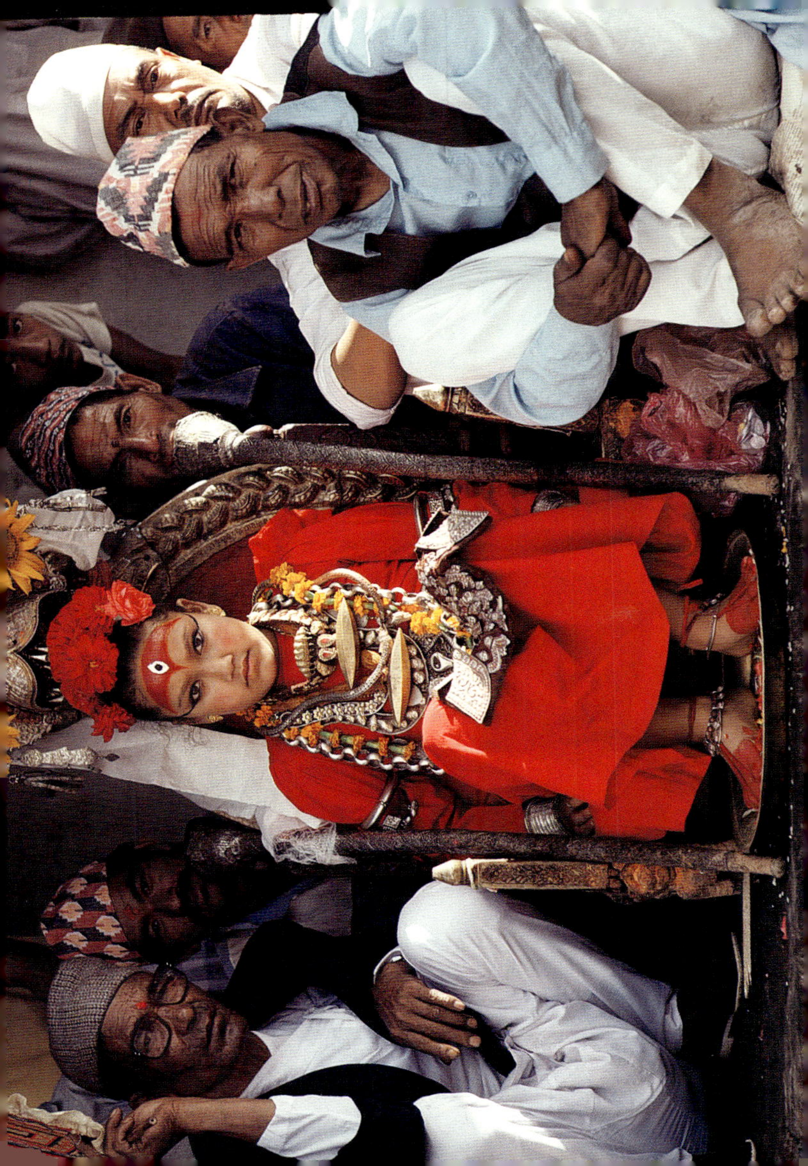

■ *No monarch has ruled since the time of the last Malla King without going to receive the Kumari's blessing every year.*

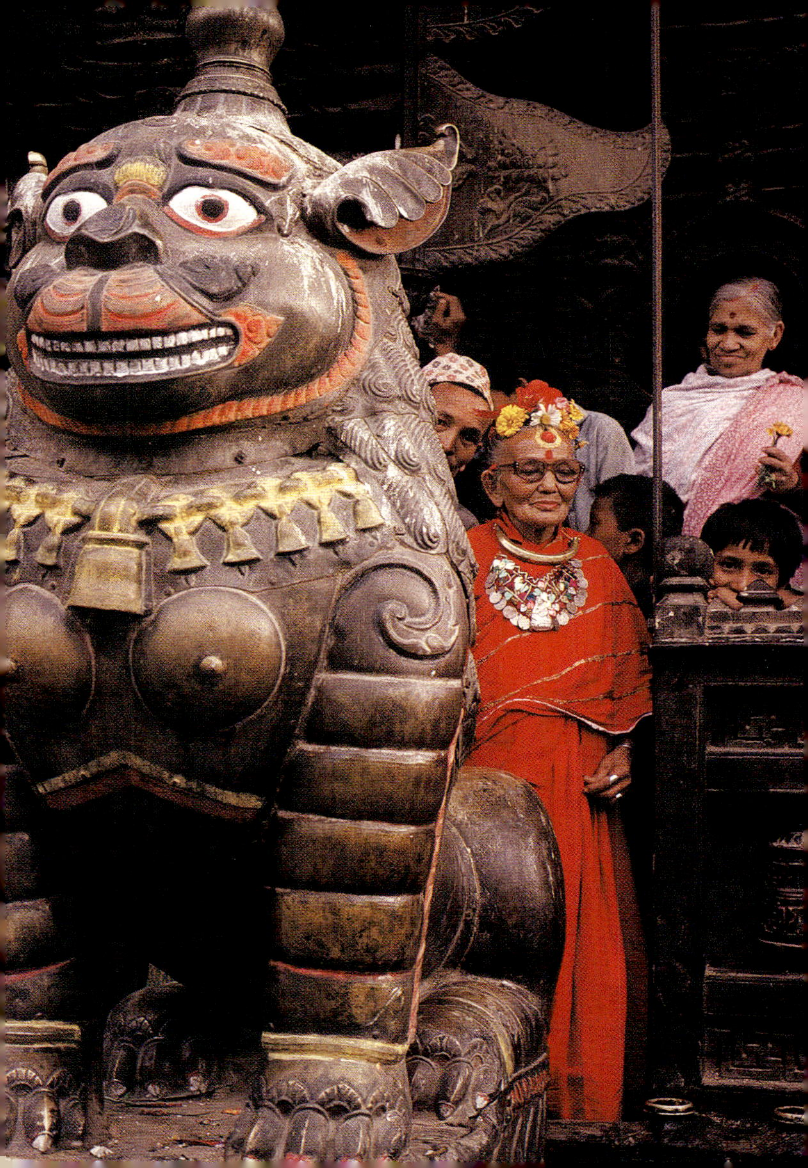

■ *The Kumaris generally give audience to the people from a window. Some, however, come before the public gaze during times of festivals.*

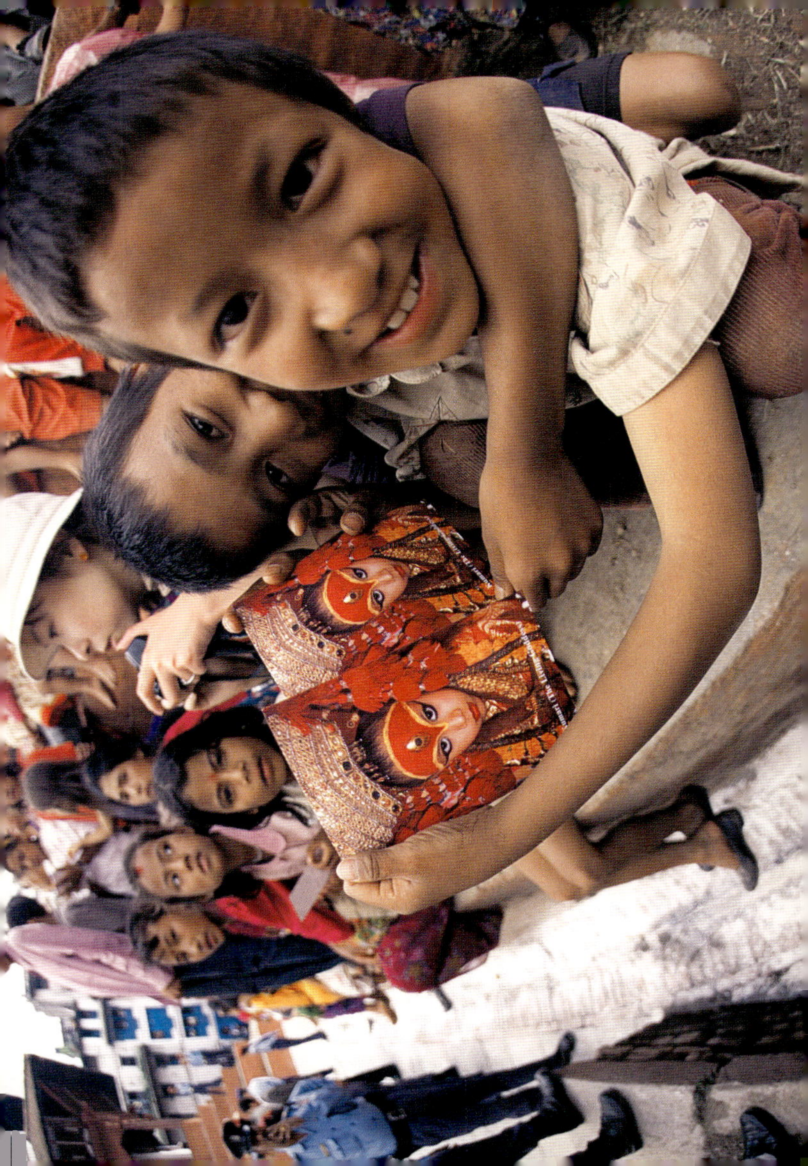

■ *As people line up to catch a glimpse of the Kumari, children who would in normal circumstances be her playmates turn into her devotees.*

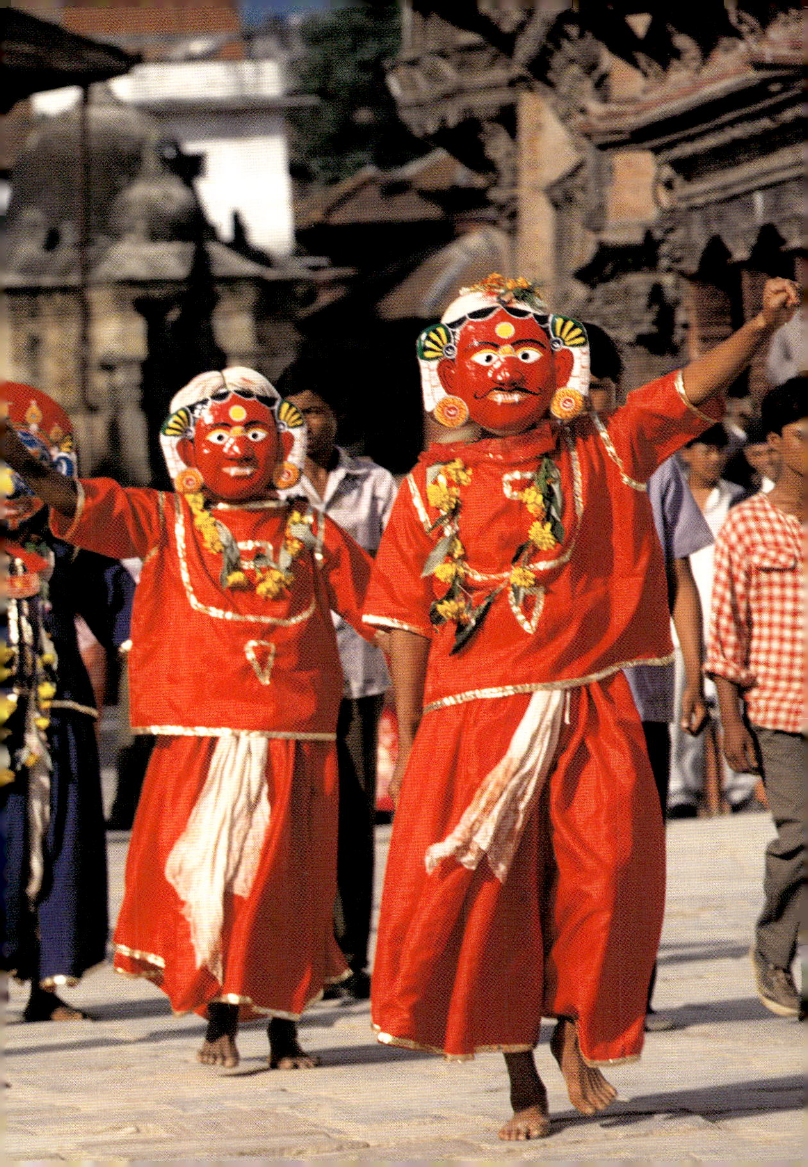

■ *Masked dancers, richly caparisoned, evoke the festive mood and represent the divine faces that are a constant theme of Nepal's religious life.*

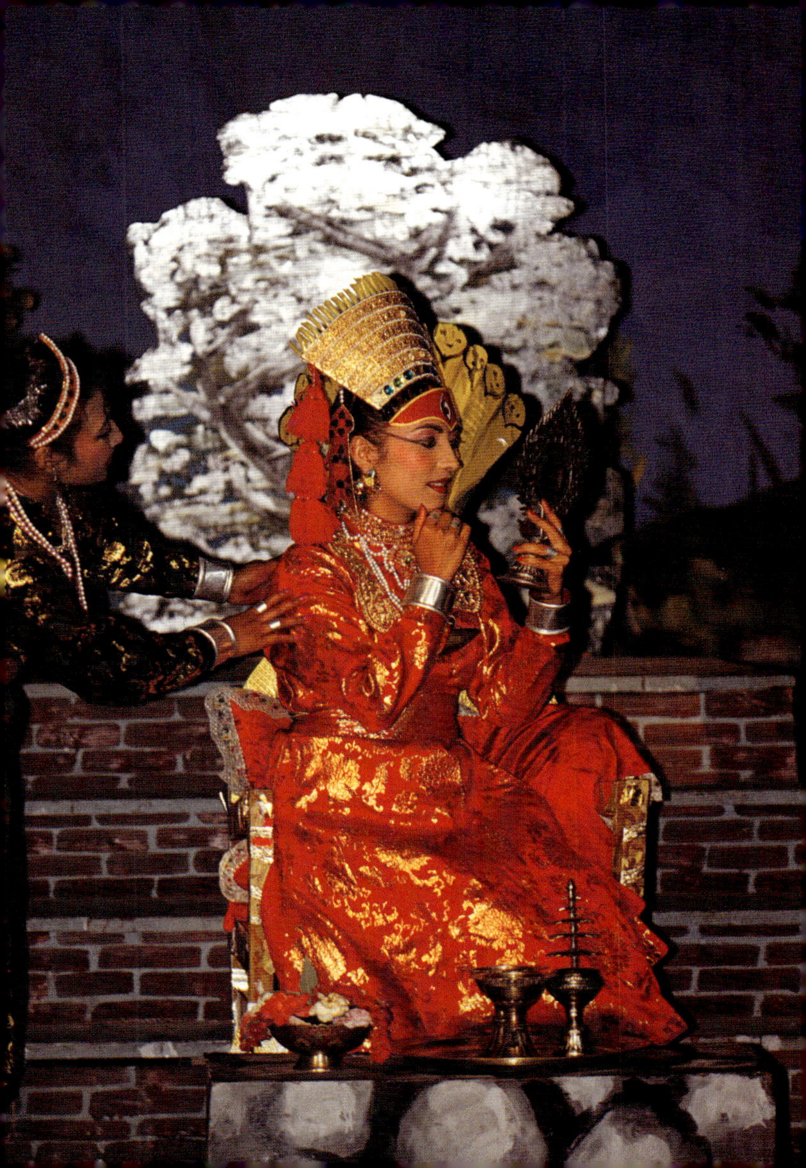

■ *During the tenth day of the festival of Dasain or Dussehra, the virgin goddess is worshipped as Durga, one of the manifestations of the female principle or* Shakti.

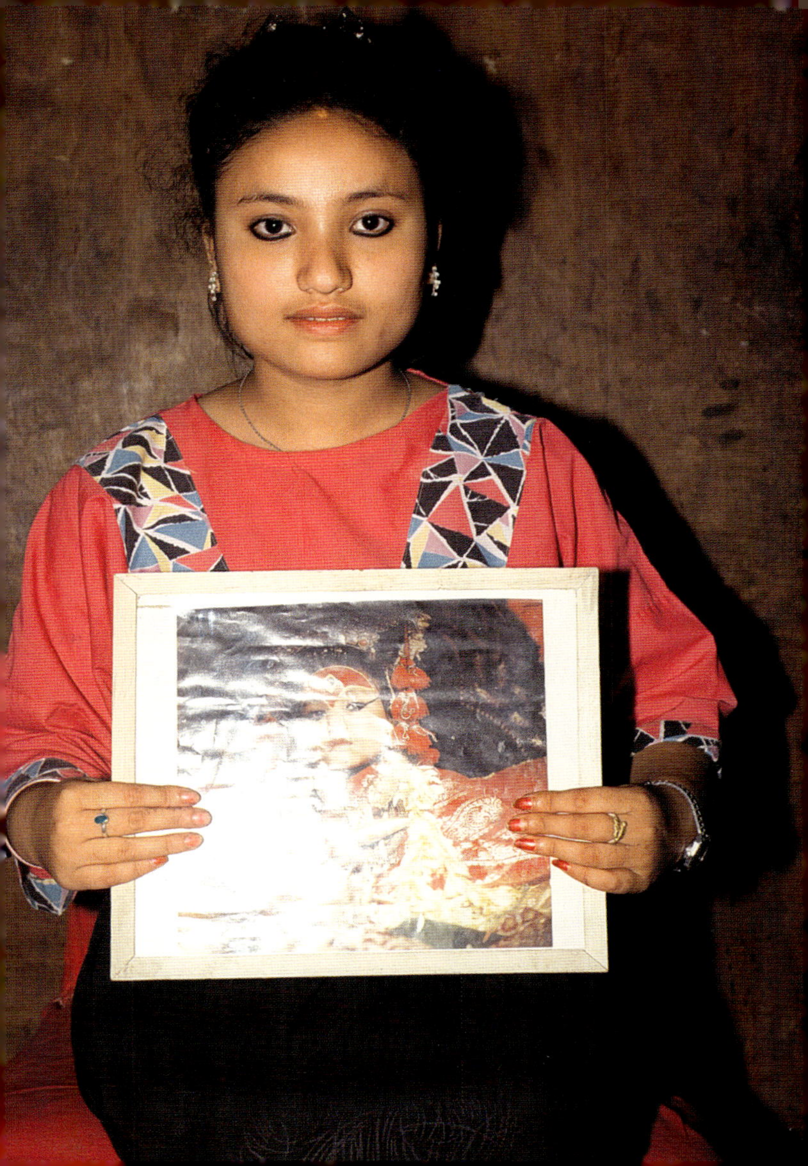

■ *A former virgin goddess holds up a photograph of the time when she was a Kumari. Kumaris are dethroned when they attain puberty.*

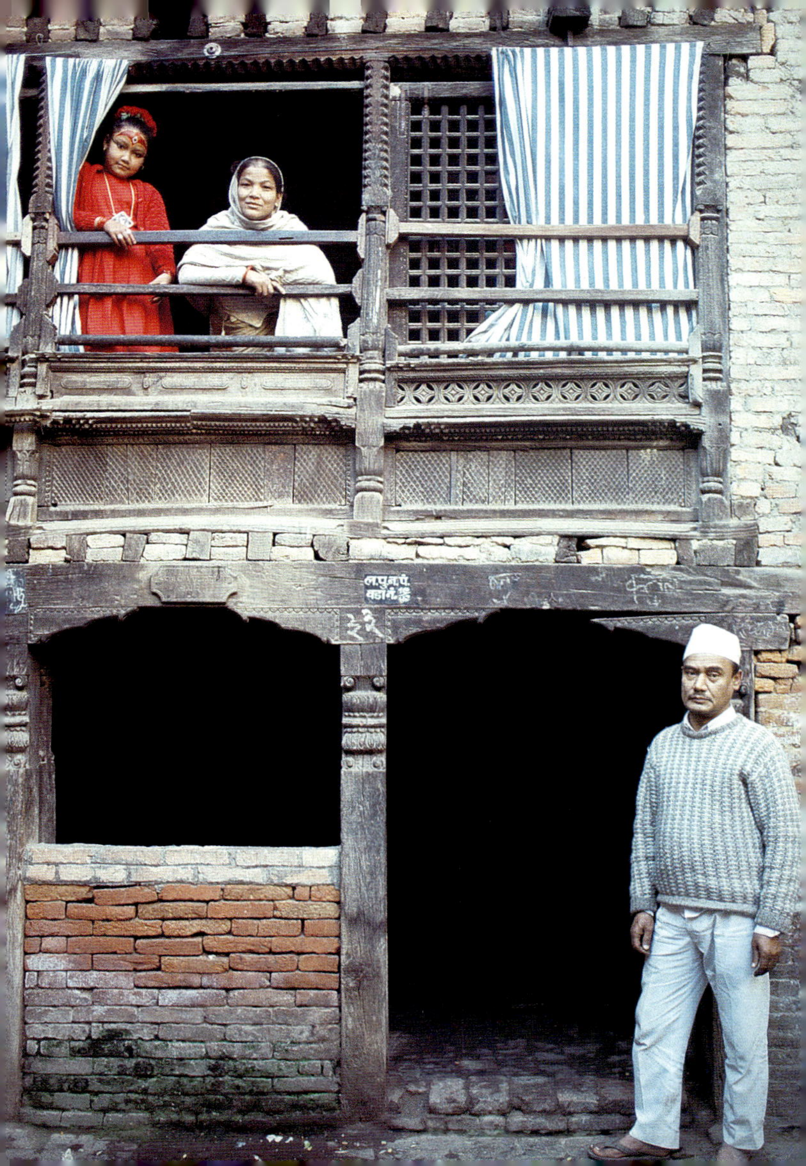
ल.पु.न.पं.
वडा नं.

■ *A young Kumari peeps from her house. Kumaris retain no ties with their house and household after the Goddess Taleju has entered them.*

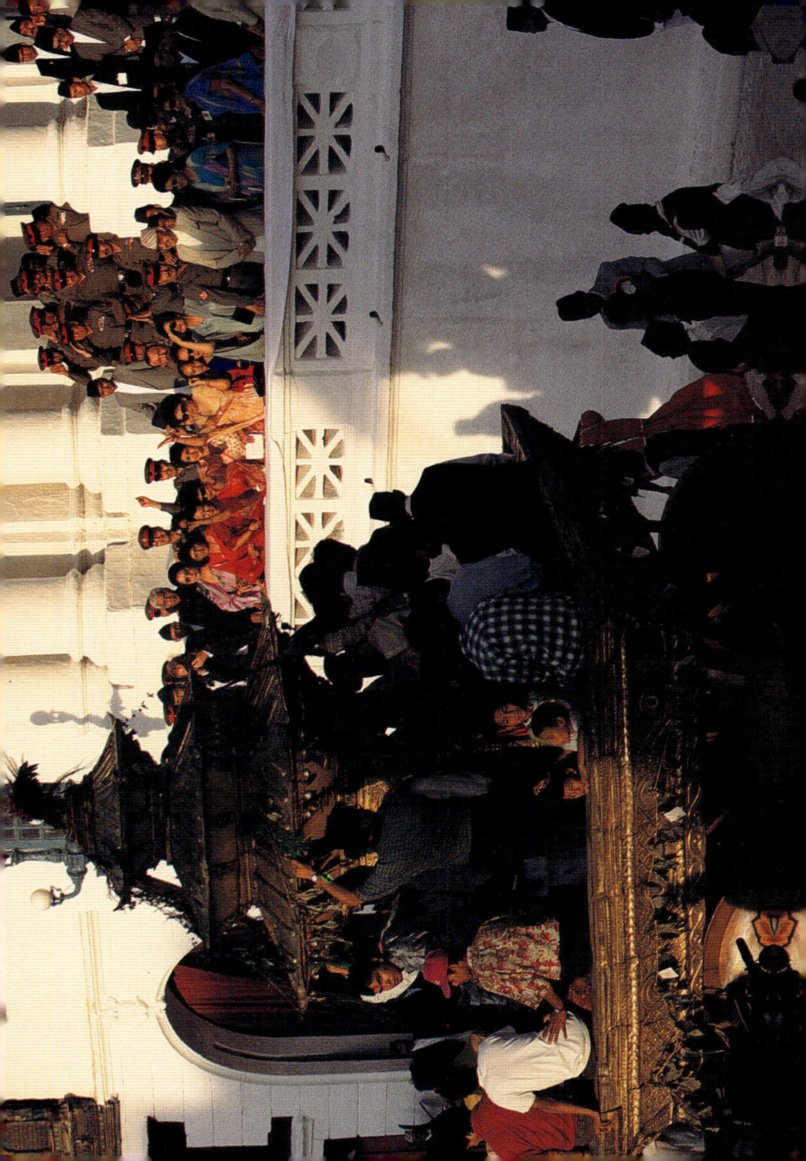

■ *The Kumaris' temple is crowded by onlookers. Modern materialism has not been able to make any incursions into the belief in Kumari worship.*

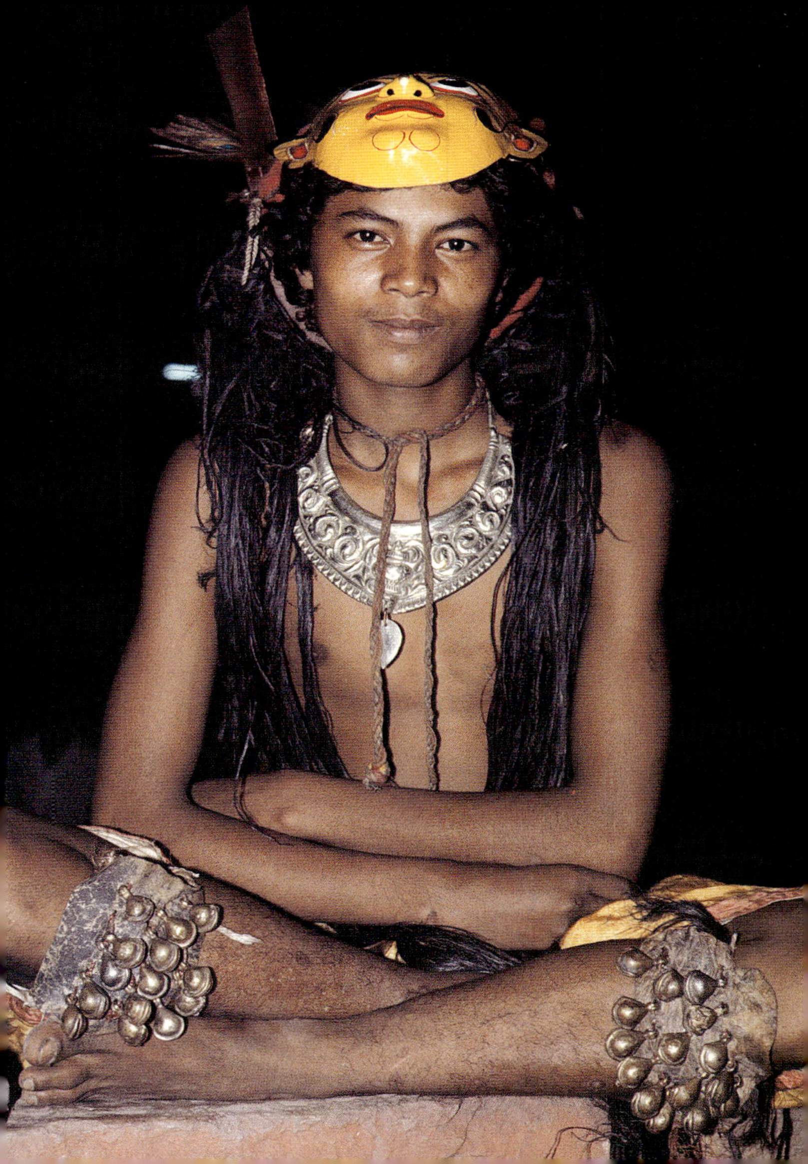

■ *A young man sits in the classic lotus posture. He has* ghunghrus, *dancing bells, on his legs and a mask that he has put on his head.*

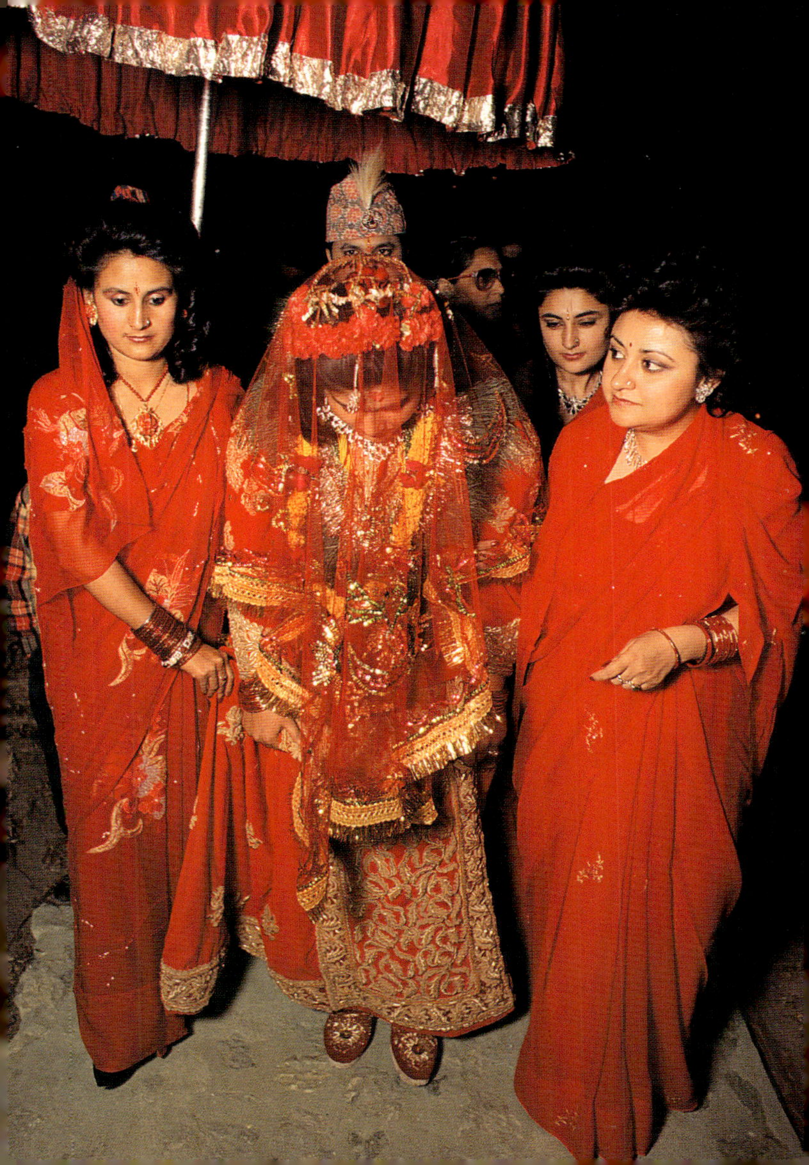

■ *The young girl is the focus of this procession. Red is an auspicious colour associated with fertility and the unrelieved red attire is believed to symbolise it.*

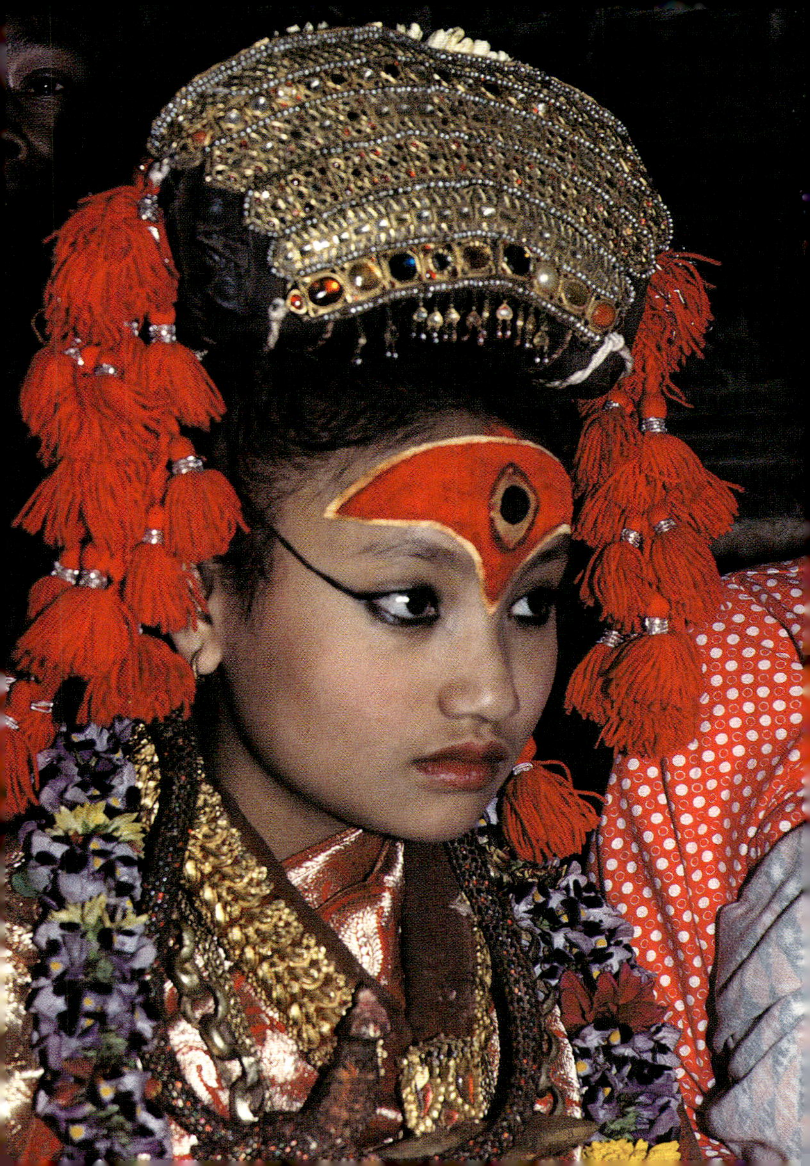

■ *A vigorous paint job makes young girls into virgin goddesses. The eyes are made to dominate the face, and the dress is fit for a queen.*

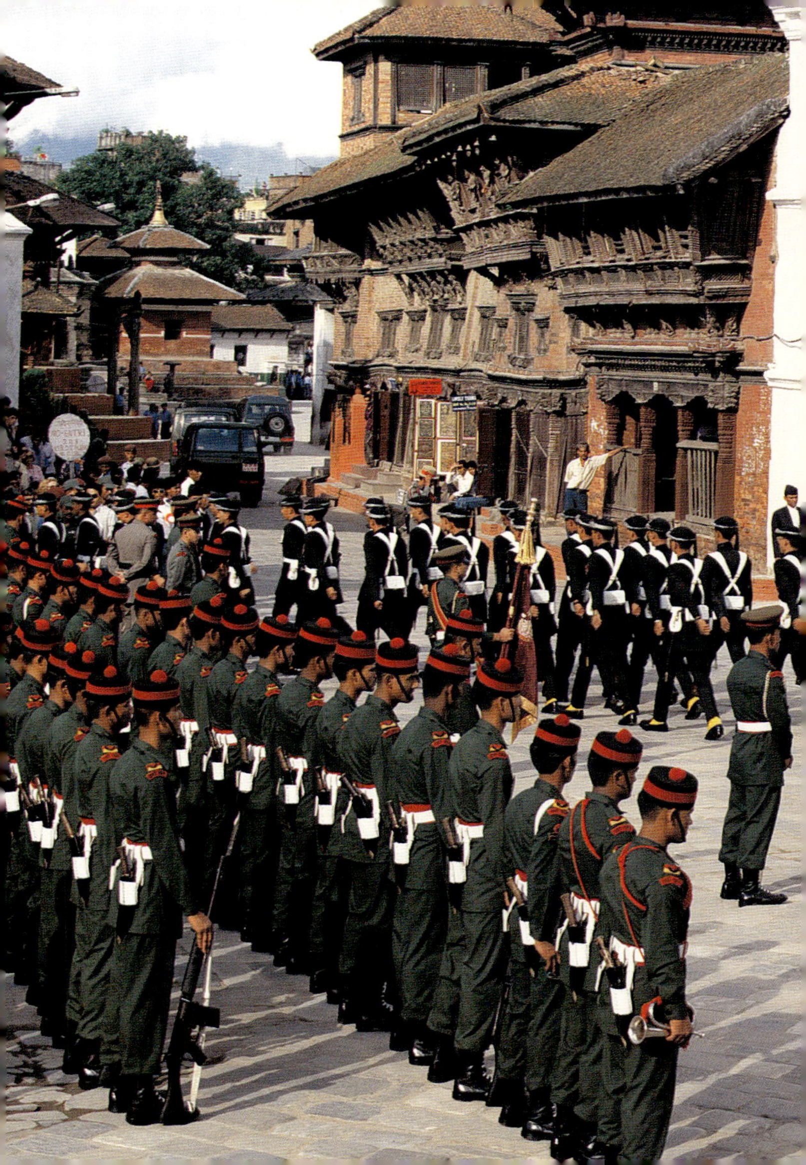

■ *Before the arrival of the Nepalese king at the Kumari Ghar, substantial security is present. Here, troops stand in formal guard at a courtyard.*

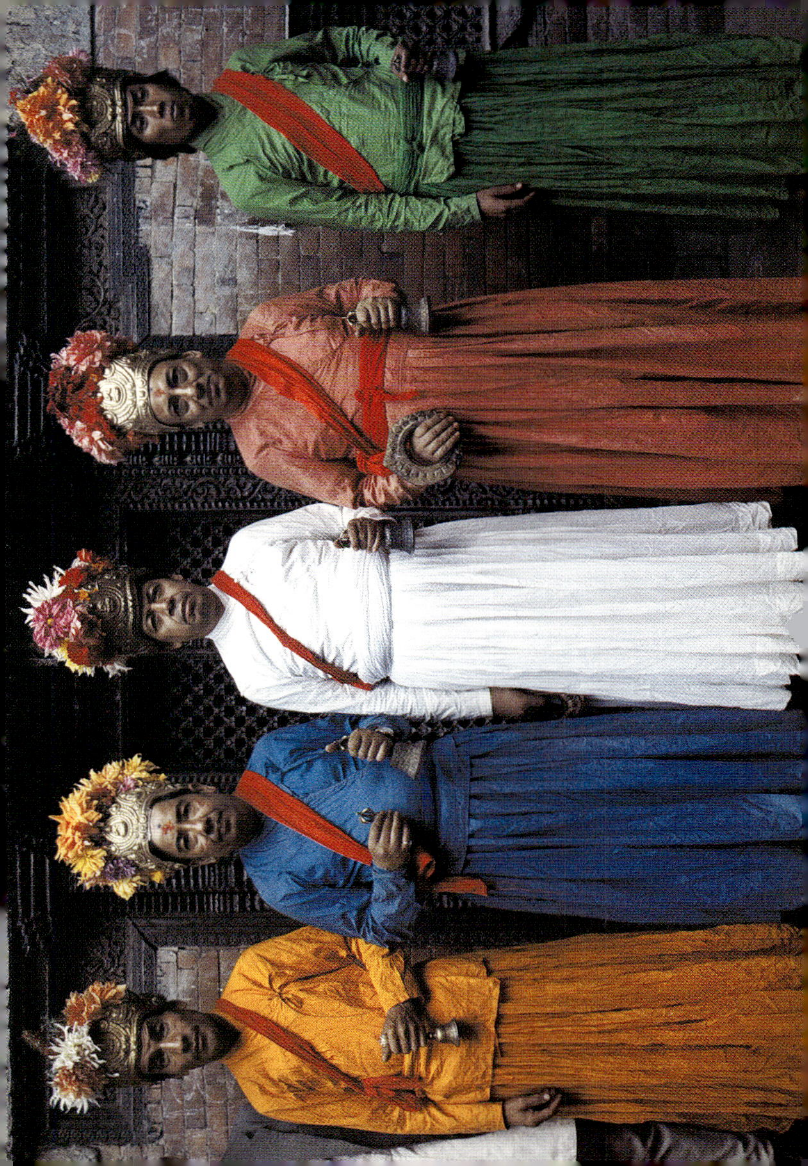

■ *A courtly line of noble priests who are responsible for selecting the Kumaris. The inspection is tough and includes tests of bravery.*

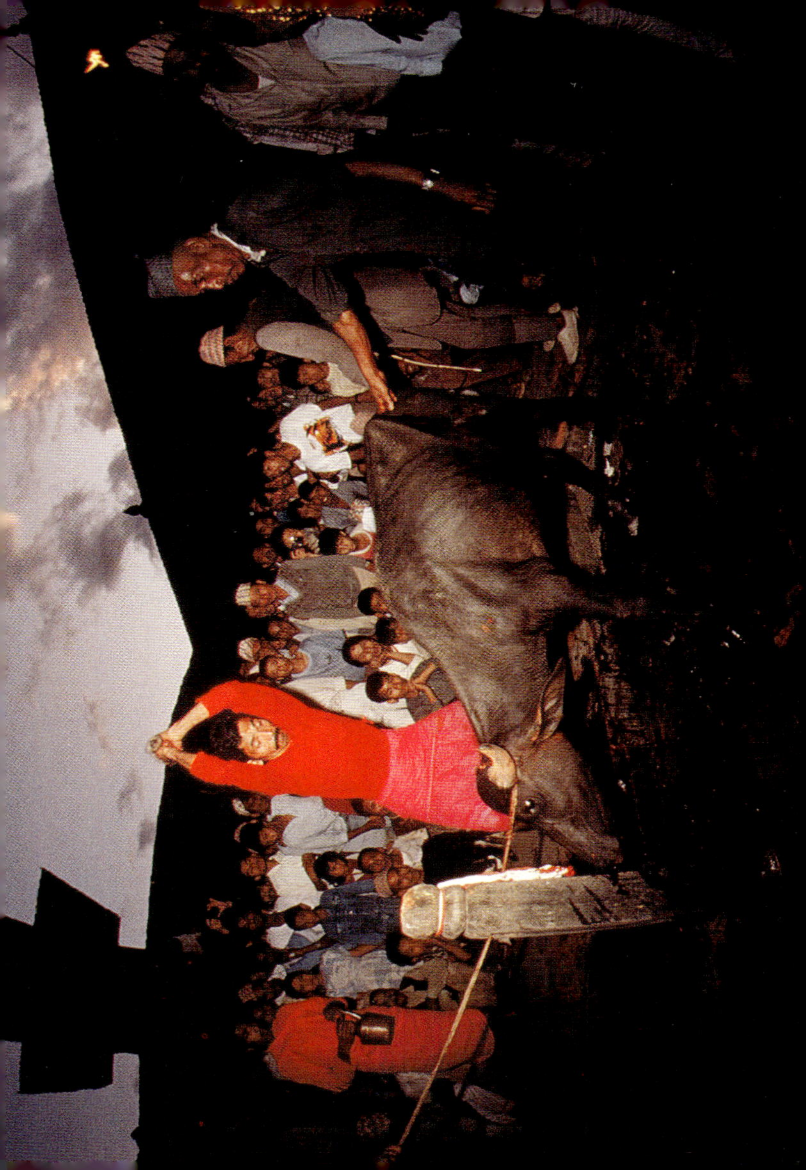

■ *On Mahashtami Day during Dasain, the Goddess is honoured with ritualistic animal sacrifices. The rituals sometimes form part of the selection procedure for a Kumari.*

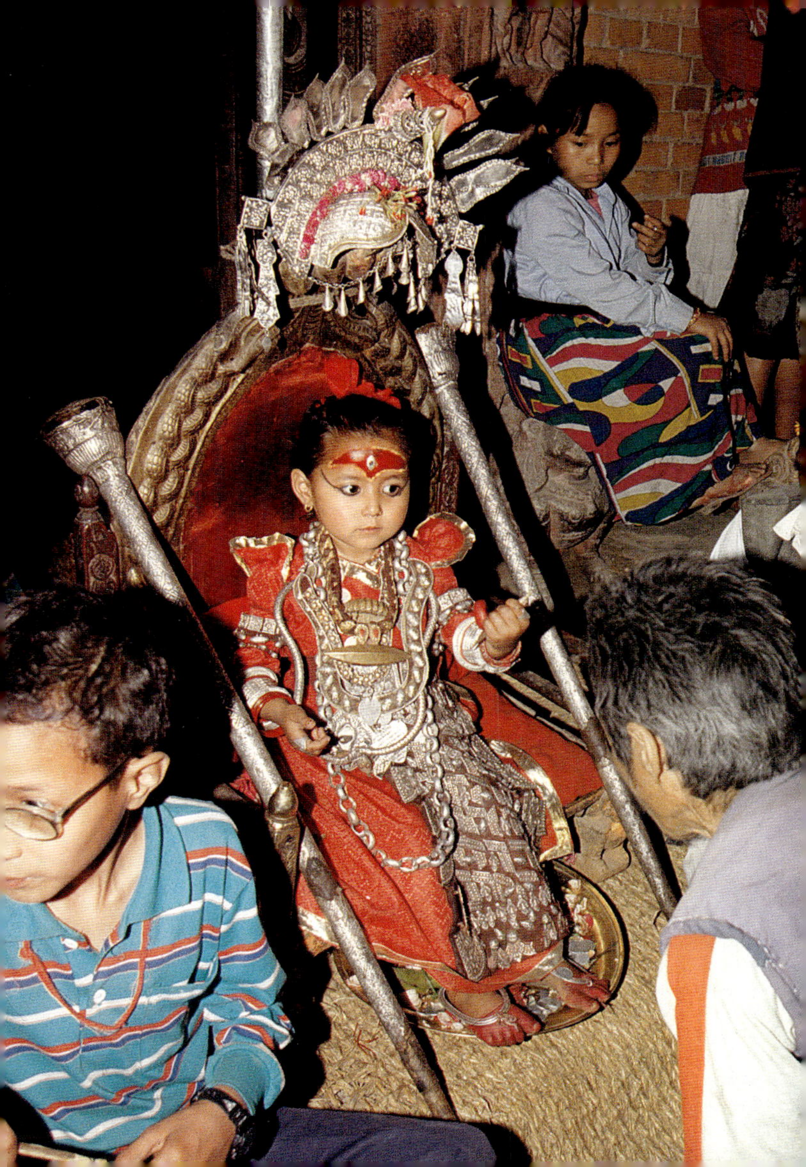

- *A young virgin goddess on her seat*
- *Page 1:* The young goddess sits on her chair.
- *Pages 2-3:* A Kumari is resplendent in her regal attire.